For the Love of God Stop Healing & Just Living

How to Stop Fixing Yourself and Finally Start Living Your Life

Debra Wilson

For the Love of God, Stop Healing & Just Start Living

By Debra Wilson

©2025 Debra Wilson

All rights reserved.

No part of this publication may be reproduced, stored in a retrieval system, or transmitted in any form or by any means without prior permission of the author.

Published by DFW Publishing

Printed in the United States of America

ISBN 979-8-9941758-2-8

Contents

Dedication	1
Acknowledgements	3
Author's Note	5
Introduction	7
1. The Endless Fix	9
2. Avoidance Dressed As Peace	13
3. Emotional Agility	17
4. Boundaries Without Bitterness	19
5. Access Revoked	23
6. Lessons From the Fire	27
7. Living Is Healing	29
Closing Reflection	33
About The Author	37

To the younger me,

for taking all the bumps and bruises

so I could be the woman I am today.

Acknowledgements

To my babies—

each one of you who stood by me and grew with me as I was learning who I was, who I needed to be for you, and who I ultimately needed to be for myself. You are my why, my heart, and my greatest reflection.

Author's Note

This book was not written from a place of crisis, confusion, or active healing. It was written from clarity. From presence. From the quiet confidence that comes when you realize you are no longer trying to survive something — you are simply living.

There comes a point when you stop asking, "What's wrong with me?" and start recognizing what has been right with you all along. God was never absent. Peace was never postponed. Life was never waiting on your perfection.

This book exists because I've learned that waiting to be fully healed before living can quietly become another form of delay. Not because healing is wrong — but because healing and living were never meant to be separate. Scripture tells us that God is near to the brokenhearted, not that He requires us to be fully restored before we move forward. His presence does not arrive at the finish line. It walks with us in the middle.

If you are reading this, you may be someone who has done the work. You've reflected. You've processed. You've prayed. You've examined your heart deeply — maybe even endlessly. And while there is wisdom in self-awareness, there is also a moment when constant introspection becomes a holding pattern. A place where you know a lot, but move very little.

This is not a call to strive harder or fix yourself faster. It is an invitation to step forward without needing to resolve every question first. To trust that obedience does not require complete understanding. To remember that faith is lived, not analyzed.

God does not wait for us to become someone else before He walks with us. He meets us as we are and then invites us to move. Healing continues as we live. Strength is revealed as we act. Peace settles as we trust.

This book is not the conclusion of a journey. It is the foundation. It is the permission to move. What comes next will speak to discernment, authority, and purpose — but this moment is about presence. About recognizing that you are already held, already guided, already capable of living fully in God.

So, take a breath. Release the pressure to arrive. You are not behind. You are not unfinished. You are already in motion. And that is more than enough to begin.

Keep healing, keep learning — but above all else, keep living.

With love and gratitude

Debra

Introduction

You know, people talk about healing like it's this grand destination you finally reach when everything makes sense, and nothing hurts anymore. I used to think that too — that if I just prayed enough, journaled enough, went silent enough, or forgave enough, I'd wake up one morning completely healed. Whole. Done.

But that's not how this works.

Healing doesn't come from waiting, or avoiding, or hiding. Healing comes from living. From falling down, standing up, forgiving yourself, and moving on. From realizing that sometimes the only way to get through it is to go through it.

I don't think we ever 100% heal — not in this life. But I do think we learn to live differently. We learn to love ourselves more, to protect our peace without losing our heart, to say "no" without guilt and "yes" without fear. We learn that we can be okay even if things didn't go how we planned.

I've been through a lot — as a woman, a mother, a leader, a daughter, and a fighter. Life taught me that every burn, every heartbreak, every setback was a class I didn't sign up for but had to take anyway. I didn't always pass on the first try, either. But I learned. I grew.

And eventually, I realized that my peace wasn't in the absence of pain — it was in how I handled it.

That's what this book is about. It's not a step-by-step on how to heal. It's not a list of affirmations or fancy advice. It's just my truth — real reflections from a woman who stopped trying to heal her way out of life and started living her way through it.

If you're reading this, maybe you're tired too. Maybe you're exhausted from trying to be perfect, from always trying to fix yourself, from running from people, or from chasing some idea of peace that feels just out of reach.

I get it.

But here's what I want you to know — you don't have to wait until you're healed to live. You don't have to close yourself off to protect yourself. You don't have to be cold to be calm. You can be soft and strong, kind and wise, healed and still human.

Because peace doesn't mean avoiding the fire — it means knowing you can walk through it and still come out whole.

So for the love of God, stop healing. Just start living.

Chapter One

The Endless Fix

Somewhere along the way, we were taught that being human meant being broken. That if something hurt, lingered, or didn't make sense, it must be something we needed to fix. The world is loud with solutions. Heal this. Release that. Work through this trauma. Set this boundary. Protect your peace. Improve yourself. And while none of those things are bad, they quietly send one dangerous message: who you are right now isn't enough.

I didn't notice it at first, but I was living in constant repair mode. Always adjusting. Always correcting. Always searching for the next version of myself that would finally feel whole. I tried new routines, new habits, new books, new prayers. And for a season, those things helped. They stretched me. They sharpened me. But eventually, I realized I wasn't healing anymore. I was hiding.

Healing became my shield. As long as I stayed busy fixing myself, I didn't have to sit with the truth that life doesn't always offer closure, clarity, or clean endings. I thought peace meant control. I thought healing meant perfection. I thought maturity meant never being affected again. What I didn't understand was that it was okay to live and still be in progress.

There came a moment when I had to ask myself a hard question: "You've been fixing for years, but are you actually living?" That question stopped me in my tracks. Because the honest answer was no. I was always reaching for what I thought I should become, instead of standing fully in who I already was. I was postponing joy until I felt more healed. Postponing rest until I felt more stable. Postponing life until I felt ready.

What I've learned since then is this: healing is not about finishing yourself. It's about learning how to move through life without letting pain dictate the pace. You can laugh and still have scars. You can love deeply and still be cautious. You can thrive while you're still figuring things out. Growth doesn't require you to erase what you've been through. It asks you to carry it with wisdom instead of shame.

Some of the most powerful lessons I've ever learned didn't come from self-help books or perfectly worded quotes. They came from real moments. From walking through fire and not turning bitter. From crying when I needed to and still showing up the next day. From praying when I didn't have answers and trusting anyway. From choosing to stay present instead of waiting to become "better."

I stopped chasing perfection and started choosing presence. I stopped treating healing like a destination and started seeing it as something that happens while you live. Every time I woke up and kept going, healing was already taking place. Quietly. Steadily. Honestly.

That's where real healing lives. Not in control, but in courage. Not in fixing, but in facing life head-on. Not in becoming someone else, but in finally standing as yourself.

Reflection Time

Take a few minutes to sit with these questions before moving on. Be honest. This space is for you.

1. What are you still trying to fix that might already be healed enough for you to live with peace?

2. When was the last time you gave yourself permission to just live, without needing to improve?

3. What would it look like if you trusted that you are already enough, right now?

Chapter Two

Avoidance Dressed As Peace

There was a season when I thought distance was the same thing as growth. If something felt uncomfortable, I removed myself. If a relationship required too much emotional effort, I cut it off. I told myself I was protecting my peace, but looking back, I can admit I was protecting my wounds.

Avoidance has a way of sounding wise when you're tired. It dresses itself up in spiritual language and self-care phrases.

"I don't have the capacity."

"I'm guarding my energy."

"I'm choosing me."

And sometimes those statements are true. But sometimes, they're just fear wrapped in better words.

I used to believe that peace meant silence. That if I could just stay far enough away from people who disappointed me, I wouldn't have to feel the sting of it anymore. What I didn't realize was that peace doesn't come from disappearing. It comes from knowing who you are, even when the room gets uncomfortable.

Real peace looks different than what I imagined. It's being able to sit in the same space as someone who once hurt you and not feel your body tense up. It's being able to speak without needing to explain yourself. It's not pretending nothing happened. It's no longer needing resolution to move forward.

These days, I don't run from anyone. I don't block people to feel powerful. I don't rearrange my life to avoid awkward moments. If we cross paths, I can speak. I can be kind. And I can keep it moving. I don't owe anyone access to me, but I also don't owe avoidance to protect my peace.

What I've learned is that healed people don't need to perform distance. They move with clarity. They know who deserves conversation and who only gets courtesy. They understand that boundaries aren't about disappearing. They're about discernment.

I no longer confuse silence with strength. I no longer believe that cutting people off is the same as growth. Sometimes growth is simply being able to stand where you are without shrinking, reacting, or retreating.

Because healing doesn't make you untouchable. It makes you unshakable.

Reflection Time

1. Have you ever mistaken distance for peace? What was really behind your need to step away?

2. Is there a situation you avoided instead of addressing? What did that avoidance cost you?

3. What would it look like to practice peace that doesn't depend on other people changing?

Chapter Three

Emotional Agility

Emotional maturity didn't come to me all at once. It came in moments where I wanted to react and chose not to. Where I felt triggered but decided to pause. Where silence became a choice, not suppression.

There was a time when I believed expressing myself meant saying everything I felt, exactly when I felt it. If something hurt me, I addressed it immediately. If I felt disrespected, I matched energy. I thought that was honesty. What I didn't realize was that emotional honesty without emotional discipline can cost you peace.

Emotional agility is the ability to feel without being ruled by what you feel. It's knowing emotions are information, not instructions. They alert you, but they don't get to drive the situation anymore.

I had to learn that reacting doesn't always mean responding. Sometimes it means reliving old wounds in new situations. Many of my strongest reactions weren't about the moment I was in, but about moments I never healed properly. Once I understood that, I stopped asking, "Why did they do that?" and started asking, "Why did this affect me this way?"

There is power in the pause. Power in taking a breath before speaking. Power in choosing not to engage when engagement will cost you clarity. Emotional agility taught me that not every feeling needs a response, and not every response needs to be verbal.

This doesn't mean I stopped feeling deeply. It means I stopped drowning in my feelings. I learned how to sit with discomfort long enough to understand it instead of acting it out. I learned how to let emotions rise and fall without letting them leave destruction behind.

Now, when something stirs me, I slow down. I observe myself. I give myself permission to feel without permission to spiral. That kind of self-control didn't make me cold. It made me free.

Because peace isn't found in emotional numbness. It's found in emotional mastery.

Reflection Time

1. Which emotions tend to control your reactions the most?

2. When was the last time you paused instead of reacting? How did that change the outcome?

3. What would emotional control look like for you without emotional suppression?

Chapter Four

Boundaries Without Bitterness

Boundaries didn't come naturally to me. I confused silence with maturity and distance with strength. When something hurt, I withdrew completely — not to protect my peace, but to avoid discomfort. I told myself that cutting people off meant I was healed, when really, I was still reacting from pain.

I misunderstood boundaries for a long time. I thought they were walls — something you built after being hurt to make sure no one could get close enough to hurt you again. But walls don't create peace. They only create distance. Real boundaries aren't about keeping people out; they're about defining where your responsibility ends and someone else's begins.

A healed person doesn't need bitterness to be firm. You can say no with love. You can walk away without hate. You can close a chapter without tearing out the entire book. Strength doesn't require hardness, and peace doesn't require isolation.

Eventually, I had to stop reacting from old wounds and start responding from self-respect. Every time I said yes when I wanted to say no, I betrayed myself. Every time I tried to please everyone, I left pieces of myself behind.

I think back on times when I would say yes simply because I didn't want to seem difficult. I avoided conflict. I didn't want to be misunderstood. But every yes chipped away at me. I was exhausted from showing up in places my spirit had already left.

One day, the truth became unavoidable. I wasn't being kind — I was being dishonest. I wasn't being mature — I was being afraid. I wasn't keeping the peace — I was keeping myself small to make others comfortable.

That's when I understood what boundaries are really for. They aren't tools to control someone else's behavior. They are commitments to your own alignment. Boundaries don't exist to make others act right — they exist to remind you to act right toward yourself.

You see, real boundaries are quiet. They don't come with speeches, warnings, or dramatic exits. They sound like:

"I won't be available for that."

"I'm choosing something different."

"I'm not comfortable with this."

"I love you, but this doesn't work for me."

And then you stand on it.

Now, when I set a boundary, I do it calmly. I don't explain it away. I don't defend it. I don't overtalk it. I honor it. If someone doesn't like it, that's not my battle to fight. My boundaries exist to protect my peace — not my pride.

Bitterness once made me feel powerful, like I was in control, like no one could hurt me again. But bitterness is heavy. It keeps you looking backward. It ties you to the very thing you're trying to rise above.

Peace is different. Peace is light. Peace looks forward. Peace releases you from the emotional debt of other people's behavior.

When your boundaries come from peace instead of pain, everything shifts. You're not shutting people out — you're letting yourself in. You're creating a life where you don't have to heal from the same situation twice.

And here's the truth: you don't lose people when you set boundaries. You lose people who were benefiting from you not having any.

Let them go. Let the version of you who over gave rest. Let the woman you are becoming take the lead.

Because boundaries aren't the end of relationships — they're the beginning of self-respect.

Reflection Time

1. What boundary have you been afraid to set because you fear someone's reaction?

2. In what ways have you betrayed your own needs just to keep the peace?

3. How can you begin practicing gentle, firm, quiet boundaries without guilt?

4. What would your life look like if you honored your limits with love instead of fear?

5. Who becomes the strongest version of you when your boundaries are respected?

Chapter Five

Access Revoked

Not everyone who hurts you is meant to be cut off — but not everyone is meant to stay close either. It took me a while to understand that protecting my peace didn't require dramatic exits or disappearing acts. It required discernment.

For a season, I moved in extremes. If someone crossed me — even slightly — I flipped a mental switch. Off. Not blocked. Not cursed out. Just gone. I told myself that was growth. I told myself distance meant maturity.

But it wasn't growth. It was survival mode dressed up as strength.

I believed eliminating people was the safest way to keep my heart intact. I believed distance guaranteed peace. What I didn't understand yet was that peace doesn't come from cutting people off. Peace comes from knowing how to manage access, not exits.

Everybody doesn't deserve the same access to you they once had. That isn't spite — it's maturity. Access is earned through consistency, respect, and energy. And when those things change, the level of access changes too.

I used to think being the bigger person meant letting people back in just to prove I had forgiven them. Forgiveness felt incomplete unless I reopened the door. But forgiveness and access are not the same thing. I can wish you well from a distance and mean it. I can pray for your peace without inviting you back into my space.

There was a time I kept giving someone chance after chance because I wanted them to see my value. I wanted them to recognize who I was. But every time I reopened the door, I reopened the wound. I wasn't hoping for reconciliation — I was hoping for validation.

And validation is not love.

Validation is not healing.

Validation is the lie pain tells you when it wants to feel important.

You don't have to prove you're over someone by letting them back in. Maturity is knowing who belongs in your life — and at what distance. It's knowing your worth without needing someone else to confirm it.

I don't block people anymore. I don't go out of my way to avoid them either. I just move differently. You can call if you want to, but I don't have to answer. We can be in the same room, and I can speak without engaging. My peace doesn't depend on your apology anymore.

That's the freedom healing brings.

Not angry distance — intentional distance.

Not punishment — protection.

Not coldness — clarity.

I've accepted that it's not my job to teach anyone how to value me. My job is to value myself enough to stop giving discounts to people who can't afford my energy. That isn't ego. That's self-respect.

Access is a privilege. Not everyone who once had it still deserves it — and that's okay. Some people were lessons, not lifetimes. Some were chapters, not the whole book. Some were mirrors showing you who you were, not who you were meant to stay.

Here's the wisdom time gives you: you don't lose anything when you limit someone's access. You gain peace. You gain clarity. You gain yourself again.

You are not obligated to keep anyone in a space they no longer respect. Letting someone stay where they choose to be — outside your inner circle — isn't cruelty. It's alignment.

Stop reopening doors God Himself closed.

Stop giving front-row seats to people who clap for you with hesitation.

Stop granting access that costs your spirit too much to maintain.

Protect your peace.

Honor your growth.

And let the distance do what the apology never could.

Reflection Time

1. Who currently has access to you out of habit rather than alignment?

2. What would protecting your energy really look like if you stopped worrying about being "the bigger person"?

3. How can you practice forgiveness without reopening emotional entry points?

4. Where in your life do you need to shift someone from front-row access to balcony seating?

5. How would your peace change if you stopped reopening closed doors?

Chapter Six

Lessons From the Fire

Life has a way of teaching you through heat. You don't really know how strong you are until something burns you, and you have to decide whether to sit in the ashes or rise out of them.

I've touched a lot of hot stoves in my life. Some emotional, some financial, some spiritual. Each one left a mark, but every mark came with a message. Pain doesn't come to destroy you. It comes to wake you up.

I used to try living life by avoiding pain at all costs. I thought if I could keep things under control, stay quiet, stay out of the way, I could stay safe. But you can't learn anything if you never get close enough to feel the heat.

The stove has to be hot for you to know it burns. The heartbreak has to sting for you to know you deserve more. The mistake has to hurt for you to know what not to repeat. And if you're wise, you won't keep going back to touch the same fire.

I've learned that sometimes God lets the fire come not to punish us but to purify us. To remind us of who we are and what we're made of. Every trial, every loss, every closed door taught me something about myself. It showed me what I could survive.

Now, when I feel the flames rising in life, I don't panic like I used to. I remember the fires I've already walked through and how each one refined me. I'm not afraid of getting burned anymore. I just make sure I carry the lesson with me.

Because healing isn't about never touching the fire again. It's about knowing when it's time to walk away from it for good.

Reflection Time

1. Think of a time when life "burned" you. What lesson did that experience teach you?

2. Are there fires you keep returning to, hoping for a different result? What keeps drawing you back?

3. How can you begin to see past pain as something that shaped you instead of something that broke you?

Chapter Seven

Living Is Healing

And then one day, it happened. I stopped trying to heal and started living again. Not perfect living. Not peaceful every day. Just living. Breathing. Laughing. Learning.

I stopped telling myself that healing was something I had to reach before I could enjoy your life again. I stopped saying, "Once I'm fully healed, then I'll travel more, open up more, love again, trust again." I paused whole pieces of my life, waiting for a version of myself I hadn't even met yet. But one day I realized something powerful: I wasn't healing — I was waiting. And waiting was keeping me stuck in the very pain I was trying to escape.

Healing doesn't happen in silence and solitude alone. It doesn't always come from isolation, journaling, or shutting the world out. It happens in motion. It happens when you go for a walk and realize you're not crying this time. When you see someone who once hurt you and your body stays calm. When you laugh without guilt. When you breathe without heaviness. When you no longer feel the need to revisit the story just to get closure that never came.

Living is healing. Every new day is proof of that.

On one of my morning walks something small made me laugh — really laugh — and it felt strange, almost foreign. I hadn't realized how long I had been in survival mode. That laugh was my reminder that my spirit was waking back up. Healing had been happening quietly in the background while I was too busy chasing some dramatic "breakthrough" to notice.

We think healing is loud. We expect it to come with revelations, tears, shaking, release. But most of the healing I've experienced showed up quietly. Softly. Subtly. In moments I almost overlooked.

Healing is choosing gratitude on a random Tuesday. Healing is answering the phone without anxiety. Healing is waking up with a lighter chest. Healing is giving yourself grace for something you used to beat yourself up over. Healing is saying "I deserve better" and truly believing it. Healing is no longer rehearsing your hurt.

And healing is understanding that life doesn't have to be perfect for you to enjoy it.

I've accepted that peace isn't the absence of struggle. It's the presence of acceptance. It's the quiet knowing that even if life gets messy again, I've already proven that I can make it through.

Living is where healing actually happens. You don't have to be "fully healed" to start a new chapter. You don't have to erase every scar to deserve joy. You don't have to have all the answers to walk into a better season.

Sometimes the most healing thing you can do is allow yourself to enjoy what's in front of you, even if you're still stitching up the past behind you.

I don't chase healing anymore. I live it. I feel it when I choose gratitude over worry. I see it when I give grace to people who once tested me. I know it when I wake up in peace and go to bed with a clear conscience.

This is what healing looks like now. It's not loud. It's not dramatic. It's steady. It's holy. It's human.

And every time I breathe in the beauty of a simple day, I'm reminded that I made it. Not because I never broke, but because I didn't stay broken.

Reflection Time

1. In this season of your life, what does living freely look like — truly?

2. What signs of healing have been happening quietly that you haven't acknowledged yet?

3. What small joys can you welcome back into your life without waiting for the "perfect time"?

4. How can you create more space for living instead of constantly working on yourself?

5. What part of you is ready to step into life again — even if you're not "all the way healed"?

Closing Reflection

For the Love of God, Just Live

If you've made it this far, I want to thank you. Not just for reading, but for sitting with truth — your truth and mine. Because truth requires courage. It requires honesty. It requires a willingness to look at yourself without judgment and still choose to love who you're becoming.

Healing has become a trendy word in our world today. People talk about it like it's a destination, a prize, a place where the sun always shines and nothing challenges you anymore. But what nobody says is that healing doesn't look the same for everyone. Healing doesn't always feel good. Healing isn't something you complete — it's something you live.

We spend so much time trying to become the best version of ourselves that we forget the beauty of the version that's here now. The one that's already been through storms, heartbreaks, lessons, and still shows up with love in her heart. The one who survived situations that should have broken her. The one who learned, grew, adjusted, surrendered, and kept going.

That woman deserves celebration, not correction. She deserves compassion, not criticism. She deserves rest, not pressure.

I wrote this because I got tired of watching people chase perfection and call it peace. I've done it too. I've hidden behind healing like it was a job, a responsibility, a mask I needed to wear just to prove I was working on myself. But peace is not something you chase; it's something you choose. Every single day.

And you don't need a perfect version of yourself to choose peace. You just need a willing one. A present one. A version of you that shows up even when she's tired. A version that keeps trying even when she doesn't know what comes next.

Healing isn't the reward. Living is.

There's no timeline for healing. No checklist, no end date, no medal for who gets there first. There's only life — and how you decide to live it. Some days you'll feel strong. Some days you'll feel weak. Some days you'll feel both within a few hours. All of it counts. All of it matters. All of it means you're still here.

Keep living. Keep showing up to your own story. Keep loving even when it scares you. Keep forgiving even when it's hard. Keep letting life teach you, refine you, and reveal who you really are beneath all the survival.

Living will stretch you. Living will soften you. Living will heal you in ways you never expected.

You don't have to run from your past to be free from it. You don't have to pretend you're healed to be worthy of a beautiful life. You don't have to avoid love, connection, or joy while you wait for the "perfect time."

You are allowed to live now. You are allowed to feel now. You are allowed to be whole — even with a few missing pieces.

Because the truth is, healing isn't something you find. It's something that finds you while you live with honesty, faith, and courage.

So, for the love of God, stop healing. Just live. And while you do, you'll realize you've been healing all along — not through perfection, but through your willingness to keep going.

About The Author

Debra Wilson is an entrepreneur, Enrolled Agent, author, and transformational leader whose life embodies grit, grace, and forward motion. A mother of six and grandmother, she has spent more than thirty years helping individuals navigate financial, personal, and spiritual transitions with clarity and confidence.

Through Momentum Miles, Debra turned her own healing journey through movement into a broader mission focused on endurance, wellness, and rebuilding strength from the inside out. What began as a commitment to run races across the country evolved into a message of perseverance, discipline, and intentional living.

Debra is also the visionary behind the Momentum Rising Foundation, an emerging philanthropic initiative dedicated to empowering individuals and families through wellness, education, and community support. Her work is grounded in the belief that momentum is the catalyst for transformation, and that progress does not require perfection, only movement.

Whether she is serving clients through Premier Tax, mentoring professionals, writing, or investing in her community, Debra leads with authenticity, wisdom, and a deep sense of calling. *For the Love of God, Stop Healing & Just Start Living* is her debut release in a growing collection of reflections centered on truth, presence, and the courage to live fully.

Reflections

On the next pages, write what you're ready to release so you can start living again.

www.ingramcontent.com/pod-product-compliance
Lightning Source LLC
LaVergne TN
LVHW041559070526
838199LV00046B/2050